What Are Patterns in Space?

HOUGHTON MIFFLIN HARCOURT

PHOTOGRAPHY CREDITS: COVER (bg) ©Christophe Lehenaff/Photononstop/Corbis; 3 (c) ©Spirit of America/Shutterstock; (b) ©VanHart/Shutterstock; 4 (b) ©Photodisc/Getty Images; 5 (r) ©Anton Balazh/Shutterstock; 6 (l) ©Albrecht Weiber/imagebroker RF/age fotostock; (r) ©P. Broze & A. Chederros/ONOKY - Photononstop/Alamy Images; 6 (tc) ©sebikus/Shutterstock; 7 (t) ©Joseph Sohm-Visions of America/Stockbyte/Getty Images; 9 (r) ©Stuart Fox/Getty Images; (l) ©gorillaimages/Shutterstock; 10 (b) ©PhotoDisc/Getty Images; 11 (l, r) ©Clifford Rhodes/Alamy Images; 14 (t) ©M. Delpho/Arco Images GmbH/Alamy Images; 16 (b) ©Tristan3D/Shutterstock; 17 (t) ©IMAGINA Photography/Alamy Images; 18 (t) ©Christophe Lehenaff/Photononstop/Corbis; 20 (t) ©Orla/Shutterstock; 21 (b) ©Digital Vision/Getty Images; 22 (t) ©Digital Vision/Getty Images

Printed in Mexico

ISBN: 978-0-544-07320-3

4 5 6 7 8 9 10 0908 21 20 19 18 17 16

4500608014   A B C D E F G

Be an Active Reader!

Look at these words.

rotates	orbit	moon phases
axis	tide	constellation

Look for answers to these questions.

What causes day and night?

How does Earth move?

What are shadows, and how do they change?

What causes the seasons?

What is the moon?

How do the sun, Earth, and the moon work together?

Why does the shape of the moon seem to change?

What are the moon's phases?

Why do the constellations seem to move?

What do we know about other planets?

What else is found in space?

What causes day and night?

It's light outside when you wake up in the morning. It stays that way throughout the day. Every night, it gets dark and stays that way until the next morning. This pattern repeats every day. Let's find out why.

Earth rotates, or turns. It makes one full turn every 24 hours. During that time, one part of Earth faces the sun. It's day in that part of the world. The other part faces away from the sun. It's night in that part.

While you are going to school during the day, students on the other side of the world are sleeping at night.

How does Earth move?

Earth rotates on an axis, an imaginary line that runs through Earth from the North Pole to the South Pole.

To visualize what an axis is, imagine sticking your left forefinger into the hole of a pitted olive and holding the olive upright. Your finger is the axis, and the olive is Earth. Now bend your wrist until the axis (your finger) is leaning to the left a bit. Like the olive, Earth tilts on its axis.

As Earth rotates on its axis, it also revolves, or moves in a curved path, around the sun. How long does that take Earth? A year. Every 365 days, Earth travels around the sun in an orbit. An orbit is the curved path that an object takes around another object in space.

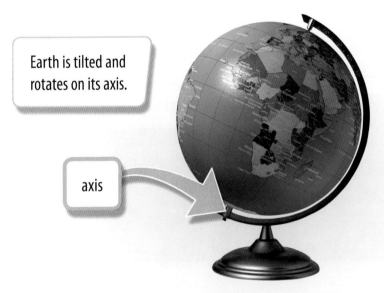

Earth is tilted and rotates on its axis.

axis

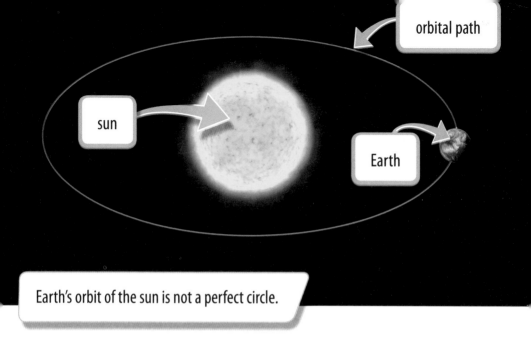

sun

orbital path

Earth

Earth's orbit of the sun is not a perfect circle.

The average distance between Earth and the sun is 150 million kilometers (km), or 93 million miles (mi). This measure is an average, because the orbit that Earth follows is not a perfectly round circle. Instead, Earth's path is more like a slightly stretched-out circle. The sun sits just off the center of the "circle."

What does the distance between Earth and the sun mean in terms of the sun's position? The distance changes during the year, depending on where Earth is in its orbit. At the closest point, Earth and the sun are about 147 million km (91 million mi) apart. At the farthest point, they are about 152 million km (95 million mi) apart.

What are shadows, and how do they change?

A shadow is a dark area or shape that's created when an object comes between the sun's rays and a surface, such as the ground.

Shadows change throughout the day. You can observe this yourself. Go outside in the morning and stand in a place where the sun is shining. Then look down and note where your shadow is. Go back outside at noon to that same spot, and look at your shadow again. What do you observe?

Shadows change as the day goes by. They're long in the morning and afternoon because the sun is low in the sky. At noon, the sun is right over our heads, and our shadows are the shortest.

Compare the shadows in the photos below. Which photo was taken closer to the middle of the day? Explain your reasoning.

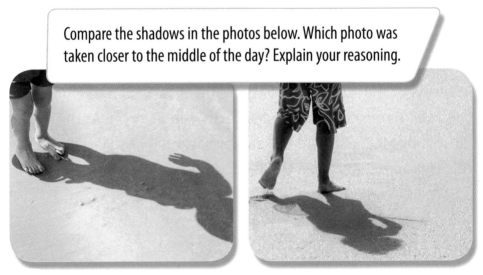

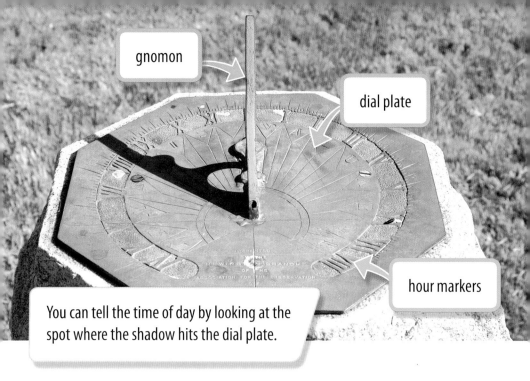

gnomon

dial plate

hour markers

You can tell the time of day by looking at the spot where the shadow hits the dial plate.

Sundials use shadows cast by the sun to show the time of day. The Egyptians created the first sundials as early as 3500 BCE.

A sundial consists of a bottom piece, called a dial plate, which is made of metal, wood, or stone. Small lines on the dial plate show the hours of the day. A sundial also has a sticklike part that stands up from the plate at an angle. The sticklike part, called a gnomon, casts a shadow on the plate. As Earth rotates, the gnomon's shadow moves around the dial. The shadow falls on a new line every hour.

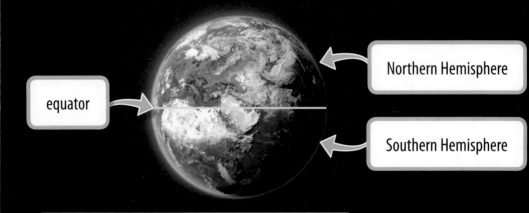

equator

Northern Hemisphere

Southern Hemisphere

The area from the equator to the North Pole is the Northern Hemisphere. The area from the equator to the South Pole is the Southern Hemisphere.

What causes the seasons?

The four seasons are spring, summer, fall, and winter. Did you know that the seasons change because of Earth's tilt on its axis and its orbit around the sun?

An imaginary line divides Earth into two parts. That line is the equator. The part above the line is the Northern Hemisphere. The part below the line is the Southern Hemisphere.

Because Earth is tilted on its axis, the Northern Hemisphere is angled toward the sun for about half of the year. During this time, the Northern Hemisphere receives more direct sunlight than the Southern Hemisphere does.

When the Northern Hemisphere is tilted toward the sun, that part of Earth has its warmest season, which is summer. Think about what's happening in the Southern Hemisphere. It's tilted away from the sun. At the same time that it's summer for you in the Northern Hemisphere, it's winter for the people who live in countries below the equator. In other words, the seasons are caused by changes in how light from the sun hits the different parts of Earth.

When it is winter in one hemisphere, it is summer in the other hemisphere.

What is the moon?

The moon is a satellite of Earth. A satellite moves around another larger object in space. There is no air, wind, or liquid water on the moon. Much of the surface is covered in craters, which are pits, or sunken areas. The craters are caused by other natural bodies of matter that have crashed into the moon. When these other natural bodies of matter crash into the moon, they break into rocks.

The moon is only about one-fourth the size of Earth. The moon looks large because it is the closest object to us. In fact, after the sun, the moon is the brightest object in the sky, but it is reflecting the sun's light, not making its own.

Craters cover the moon's surface, but there are also mountains and large, flat plains called *maria*. This is a Latin word meaning "seas."

Earth has a force called gravity. Gravity pulls things toward Earth's center and keeps you from floating around above the ground. The moon also has its own gravity.

Earth and the moon are about 384,400 km (238,900 mi) away from each other. The two are close enough that the moon's gravity pulls Earth toward the moon. The pull affects the water level in the ocean. The rising and falling of the water in the ocean is called the tide. Each day, there is a high tide, when the water level is highest, and a low tide, when the water level is lowest.

If you live near the ocean, you can look in a newspaper or online to find out when the high and low tides are every day.

high tide

low tide

Gravity is what makes a ball come down after you throw it up in the air.

How do the sun, Earth, and the moon work together?

Let's review for a moment. You know that Earth rotates once on its axis every 24 hours, which is one day. You also know that Earth's orbit around the sun takes a year. Now let's add the moon. The moon rotates on its own axis. One rotation on the moon's axis takes a month. The moon also revolves around Earth in the same amount of time. That's why you always see the same side of the moon.

What keeps the sun, Earth, and the moon from colliding or floating off into space? Gravity! It's the force that keeps them in place.

The sun, Earth, and the moon work together as a system. A system is a set of things that work together as parts of a whole. Without each part, the system would not function, or work. People, plants, and animals depend on the sun for light and warmth. What would happen if the sun were no longer part of the system? What about the moon? How would the absence of the tides affect the animals and plants that live in the ocean?

Facts About the Sun, Earth, and Moon System		
	Size	Motion
Sun	1,391,000 km (864,400 mi) in diameter	• Center of revolution of other objects in the solar system
Earth	12,756 km (7,926 mi) in diameter	• Rotates once every 24 hrs • Orbits sun once about every 365 days
Moon	3,475 km (2,159 mi) in diameter	• Rotates once about every 27 days • Orbits Earth once about every 27 days

Moonlight is a reflection of the sun's rays off the surface of the moon.

Why does the shape of the moon seem to change?

If you stand outside every night for a month and gaze up at the moon, the shape of the moon appears to change. It doesn't really change, however. It only looks that way from where we are standing on Earth. The changes in the moon's appearance are called moon phases.

The moon reflects the light from the sun. As the moon revolves around Earth, one half of the moon is always lighted. What we see depends on where the moon and Earth are in their orbits around the sun. You can do an activity to see how this works.

Find a globe, a tennis ball, a lamp or flashlight, and two friends. Work in a darkened room.

First, locate North America on the globe. Have one friend turn on the lamp or flashlight. Turn the globe so that North America is facing the light. Ask your other friend to hold the ball between the globe and the lamp or flashlight. How much of the lighted side of the ball do you see?

Keep the lamp or flashlight where it is, but ask your friend to move the ball around the globe a few inches. Now how much of the lighted side of the ball do you see?

Ask your friend to continue moving the ball around the globe and note the "changing shape" of the ball. What you see should be similar to how the moon seems to change shape!

These students are modeling phases of the moon.

Earth

moon

sun

What are the moon's phases?

There are eight phases of the moon. Of the eight, four are main phases.

New moon. The moon is between the sun and Earth, and all three objects are lined up. The lighted side of the moon is facing away from us, so we can't see it.

Full moon. Earth is between the moon and the sun. We're facing the entire lighted side of the moon, so we see what looks like a full circle. The side that is not lighted is facing away from us.

First quarter and third quarter. Sometimes known as a half-moon, each of these phases is what we see when the moon is at a 90-degree angle to the sun and Earth. We see half of the moon's lighted side.

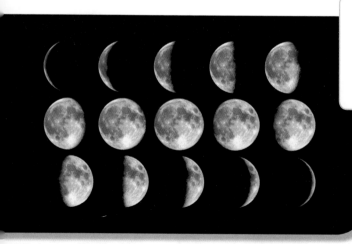

It takes about one month for the moon to go through all its phases. It takes $29\frac{1}{2}$ days.

Have you ever heard of the expression "once in a blue moon"? When there are two full moons in one calendar month—a rare thing—the second full moon is called a blue moon.

There are phases between each of the four main moon phases. When the shape is crescent and looks like a banana, we see less than a half-moon. When we see more than a half-moon but less than a full moon, the phase is called a gibbous moon.

The terms *waxing* and *waning* are used with *crescent* and *gibbous* to tell whether we can see more or less of the lighted side of the moon. Between the first-quarter moon and the full moon, we see the waxing gibbous phase. Between the full moon and the third-quarter moon is the waning gibbous phase.

The Big Dipper is part of the constellation *Ursa Major.*

Why do the constellations seem to move?

A constellation is a group of stars that seems to form a picture. We can look at the sky and identify constellations such as Cygnus the Swan, Taurus the Bull, and Leo the Lion. There are 88 constellations.

Since ancient times, people have been looking at the stars. People gave some groups of stars names because the stars seemed to form objects, animals, or characters from stories. Different cultures gave constellations different names. Today, we often use the names that the ancient Greeks and Romans used.

Just as the sun seems to move in the sky, the constellations appear to move as well. You'll see some constellations in the winter that you won't see in the summer. Some constellations that are visible in summer aren't visible in winter. Remember that Earth spins on its axis and is always moving around the sun. Your ability to see certain stars depends on what season it is—in other words, where Earth is in its orbit.

Some constellations can be seen only from above the equator. Some can be seen only from below it. Some can be seen from both places.

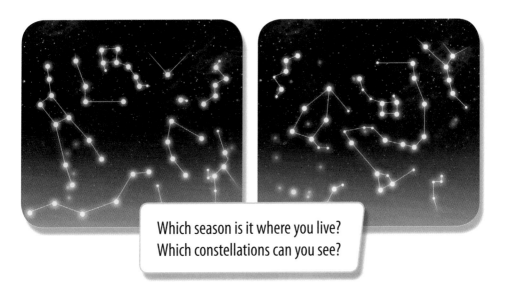

Which season is it where you live?
Which constellations can you see?

Mercury, Venus, Earth, and Mars are closest to the sun.

Earth

What do we know about other planets?

Mercury, Venus, Earth, Mars, Jupiter, Saturn, Uranus, and Neptune are all planets. They orbit the sun, and most have at least one moon.

Pluto used to be called a planet, but it has a different kind of orbit and is much smaller than the other planets. Scientists have decided that Pluto should be called a dwarf planet.

Four planets are solid and rocky and closer to the sun than the others. These planets are Mercury, Venus, Earth, and Mars. Jupiter, Saturn, Uranus, and Neptune are made up mostly of gases. Each of these planets has many moons.

Earth takes a year to orbit the sun, but the other planets take different amounts of time. That means that a day or year on Earth does not equal a day or year on Venus.

Scientists have observed that Venus's surface has plains and mountains. These scientists think that the surface was formed by lava that came out of erupting volcanoes, much like some of Earth has been formed. However, the temperature on Venus's surface is almost 482 ºCelsius (900 ºFahrenheit)! It's hot enough to melt many metals.

Venus is about the same weight and size as Earth, and its surface is rocky and solid like Earth's.

We last saw Halley's comet in 1986, and we won't see it again until 2061.

What else is found in space?

Comets, asteroids, and meteors are also in space. A comet is a small body of rock and frozen gases that orbits the sun. The gas may look like a fiery "tail" that streams away from the sun. Even before the telescope was invented, people could often see comets in the sky. The most famous comet is Halley's comet. It takes about 76 years to complete its orbit.

Asteroids are chunks of rock and metal that also orbit the sun. There are thousands of asteroids floating around in space. They are mostly found between Mars and Jupiter.

Pieces of asteroids break off and hurl into space. Sometimes the pieces come into Earth's atmosphere and begin to burn. Then they're called meteors. You might have seen a meteor shower, when many of these small glowing objects enter the atmosphere and quickly disintegrate.

Make an Argument

Some scientists think Pluto should be listed as a planet instead of a dwarf planet. What do you think? Choose a side. Use the Internet and library resources to find information about Pluto. Then debate your opinion with a partner. Use reasons and information from your research to support your opinion.

Write a Report

Use the Internet and library resources to learn about a scientist who studies space. Write a report with an introduction, body, and conclusion that explains who the scientist is, what the scientist studies, and how he or she studies it. Be sure to mention the scientist's major accomplishments and contributions to his or her field of study.

Glossary

axis [AK·sis] The imaginary line around which Earth rotates.

constellation [kahn·stuh·LAY·shuhn] A group of stars that seems to form a picture or design in the sky.

moon phases [MOON FAYZ·iz] Changes in the appearance of the moon's shape as it orbits Earth.

orbit [AWR·bit] The path of one object in space around another object.

rotates [ROH·tayts] Turns about an axis.

tide [TYD] The rise and fall in the water level of the ocean.